Dare to Dream

by
T.L. Black

Dare to Dream
by T.L. Black

ISBN: 978-1-932496-67-3

Cover and Layout designed by Antonio Marble

Manufactured in the United States of America.

Printed By Penman Publishers Cleveland, TN

DEDICATION

This book is dedicated to my son and daughter Malachi & Zeniah, may all your potential be released and your dreams be seen. Remember: believe, pursue and achieve. To Antonio Marble for the time, effort, hard work and support you have put into this project. May the passion you put into your art be reflected through these pages. And to the world, may this book inspire you to overcome fear, step out on faith and most importantly **Dare to Dream.**

TABLE OF CONTENTS

DARE TO
DREAM

I quit my job! In the middle of a recession I terminated my employment. Three months prior to my daughter's birth I dropped all benefits. And while the world calls me crazy, I dare to dream.

The year is 2008, and all of America is in panic. Jobs have been closed. Wall Street has crashed. 401K is broken. Homes are foreclosed. Families are destroyed. Food and gas prices are at an all-time high. Yet here I stand without a worry in sight. What is it that makes me gallant in such troubled times? Faith! And I write...

THE GALLANT MAN

The *Gallant* Man

I am a black man,
Strong and courageous.
Smart and creative.
Is this why the ages hate us?

Forced into chains,
They came in and raped us.
Showing no mercy,
They came to degrade us.

Stripped away our mind
While using whips to tame us,
But we were too strong
So they used ropes to hang us.

We were too superior
So they had to break us.
To make us inferior,
Masters reshaped us.

Any slave step out of line
Had to dangle,
Or lynched from the back of truck
By his ankles.

Horrific deprecation
Quenched our souls fire
But that couldn't keep us
From reaching what we desired.

We have been triumphant
Throughout the generations.
Marching tirelessly
Through hatreds infestation.

What was meant to stop us
Kept us pressing forward.
Many souls lost
But our pride was not lowered.

We fought for a purpose
And died for our beliefs.
We stood in unity
When the dogs were unleashed.

We marched gallantly
Through racial brutality.
We awoke from The Dream
To make it reality.

My culture has seen devastation in

its worse form. We have stared down the barrel of death and not even death could stop us. So why lose faith now? The worst is behind us. What is depression compared to oppression? What is a temporary struggle compared to a lifetime of poverty? Progression is demanded. When fear strikes the heart of a nation we should not fall short to the cause, but rise to the occasion. And I write...

Progression

Enough talk about recession,
Let's talk about progression
And what we can do
To prevent a great depression.

Cut back on the expenses
Of luxuries unneeded.
Discipline yourself to purchase
Only what is needed.

Tame the eye of lust
And control the spending hand.
Learn to live cheap
And preserve all you can.

Pay off all debts
The best way you know how.
Loans, too, create debt
So avoid taking one out.

Stir away from fast food
And take the time to cook.
Cut the high priced cable,
Sit down, and read a book.

Carpool to destinations
To save on gas.
Walk if it's in distance
Or buy a bus pass.

Reduce paying others
And learn to do for yourself.
By being self-reliant
You accumulate wealth.

The country's in debt
But the country's not dead.
We can make it out
If we'd just use our head.

It's time to be frugal.
It's time to live smart.
Vacation time is over.
We now must play our part.

Money should not determine
The character of our heart.
Poverty is a state of mind
And richness lies within the heart.

The economy is failing
But humanity is strong.
We have survived darker times,
So this shouldn't last long.

Worry not about investments,
But to your health, hold on.
While money comes and goes,
Life still carries on.

Do not let this steal
The purpose for your creation.
For this is the reason
You're of this generation.

You were born to endure
The mishaps of time.
Molded to perfection,
Your potential is sublime.

Life is clouded with grey skies
And love hurts at certain times,
But beyond the dark clouds
The Son still shines.

Now is the time to operate in faith. For years,

I have carried a vision of inspiring and empowering souls using my gift and talents. As days passed, the vision became clearer and clearer. Purpose was staring me in the face but I was afraid to act. I feared that if I failed I would no longer be able to provide for my family. I feared quitting my job, that paid weekly and offered great benefits, would cripple me tremendously. However, I realized I would definitely be crippling myself by not living my dream. The more I thought about following my heart the more I disliked my occupation. Pulling into the company parking lot, day by day, only added to the stress. My work performance decreased as I continuously pondered on achieving personal success. Then it hit me. The only way to be satisfied is to satisfy the desire. And I write…

PATH of GREATNESS

PATH of **GREATNESS**

How far have we come
Since the dreamer had a dream?
Are we truly free
Or is that only how it seems?

Mentally in bondage
So our mind has been deceived.
Ignorance brings death
So death will be received.

Unless we wise up
And be aware of our actions.
Make our minds whole
And do away with the fractions.

Take away the parts
That leave our life aimless.
Life without direction
Is a path marked dangerous.

So much opportunity
To make our life better.
We can move further
Once we get our act together.

The slums are no longer
Our final destination.
Prosperity is not just
A figment of our imagination.

Dreams become real
When one stops procrastinating.
Don't hold yourself back
From something more fascinating.

Build up your stamina
To be bold and courageous.
Endure through life's hardship
And difficult stages.

You can be and do whatever
By believing you can make it.
Your dreams are your own,
Don't let anyone take it.

Let no one shape it.
Let no one break it.
If you have a clear vision
Hold tight and embrace it.

Quickly write it down
Before your memory erases it.
Don't waste a good idea,
Serve it up and then taste it.

Everything you see
Originated from an image.
Even mankind
Was created in his image.

Imagine what could happen
When you put your mind to use.
Any thought imagined
Can be put to use.

If success must be driven
How far will you go?
If the world runs on knowledge
How much do you know?

Stimulate your mind
And become your own boss.
The future's yours to gain
If you can pay the cost.

And the cost is
A lot of time, a lot of work.
But if it's something that you want
You wouldn't mind the time and work.

You would spend that time to work
On your dreams and desires.
And for each achievement
You would escalate higher.

Why work for the man
When you can become the man?
Forty hours of your life
Is in another man's hand.

Forty hours of your life
You will never see again.
And your plan is to do this
Until your life ends?

What a waste of existence.
A tragic death of a purpose.
To live your whole life
Missing out on your purpose.

To die before death
And not even have a clue.
No plans for the future,
Just get up and do.

How can life be fulfilled
When you don't fill the void?
You search for a meaning
But the answer you avoid.

You drive around in circles
Going where the money is
While passing your destination
Which is where your heart is.

You head off to college
Not knowing your true purpose.
Now you have a degree
That's opposite your purpose.

You're supposed to be a doctor
But you went to study business.
Now you hate your job
Because you're in the wrong business.

When will we learn
That life is only what we make it?
If opportunity comes knocking
It's a choice whether we take it.

It is not an obligation
But it is regeneration
For a life worth living
On a path set for greatness.

LIFE'S PURPOSE

God has blessed me with an incredible gift. So for me not to use it for the good of His will would be shameful. Everyday I pass people who view life from one perspective, conventional. As if they're still plugged into the matrix, they walk blindly through life, never living to their full potential. To them, life is only about having the bigger stick. That is, the best car, house, job, schooling, and overall, presentation. But what is presentation without representation? Vanity! Nothing is wrong with attaining the best, but if done so falsely, all is wrong. Is it not vain to go after the best things of life and not the best of life? Finding and achieving purpose will fulfill your life in ways unimagined. But by skipping over purpose, your life will be affected in ways unimagined. Stress, weariness, depression, debt, frustration, complacency, dissatisfaction, and horrendous void will all result from this conventional thinking. We need to break the cycle of enslaving ourselves to dead-end commitments and pursue what our heart desires. And in pursuit, we will release our potential, giving us a purpose-filled life. And I write...

Purpose

If you have big dreams
You should shoot for the stars.
Let no noun stop you
From becoming who you are.

Because from the beginning
You were meant to be great.
Much potential is within you
To meet your own fate.

Many people live life
Not knowing who they are.
They settle for what is given;
A false truth of who they are.

PURPOSE

They may succeed in many things
And have ambition to go far.
But if they still lack happiness,
They're confused of who they are.

In order to find the truth
One must search within himself.
So what did God give you
That defines your true self?

What gift do you possess
That could heighten someone else?
Purpose isn't about you
But enhancing someone else.

Advancing someone else
Is more awarding than any wealth.
Purpose is much bigger
Then succeeding for yourself.

We have a world to change
As well as lives to save.
Don't abuse your purpose
Simply to get paid.

If it's not in God's name
Then it is done in vain.
And if it's done in vain
It will go up in flames.

Use your gift
To glorify His name
And stop wasting your talent
To self-gain and entertain.

It's OK to entertain
But back it up with a message.
In any field that we're in
We should always sew a message.

One's life is affected
By every action we choose
So make your purpose count
For all of those watching you.

Make your purpose count
For the One judging you.
What will God report
When He's evaluating you?

Will it be, "Purpose accomplished,"
Or "Mission incomplete?"
Will you live to witness
Or waste life in vanity?

Workers of iniquity
Will soon see hell.
But workers of the Lord
Will be awarded well.

So farewell to the flesh
And hello Holy Spirit.
If you're seeking out your purpose
Ask and He will give it.

We were not created
To be slaves to corporations.
The mission of our existence
Is to witness to salvation.

Be a beacon of inspiration
With a light of motivation,
Giving in to God's will
While fighting off all temptations.

Put your faith in Him,
Giving Him your whole heart,
And your life will be filled
Because your purpose then starts.

There are so many people searching for the meaning of life, as well as those seeking their individual purpose. My personal belief, pertaining to life's meaning, derives from my spiritual intuition. As a child of God, it is my job to witness to the truth. To expand His kingdom on earth, as it is in heaven, using the gift and talents He has provided. We are solely here to represent Him and enjoy the goodness of life. We represent our Creator by building our character around His word. By being hearers and doers of His word, we walk the kingdom life. And I write...

Kingdom Life

As a child, I walked like a child.
I talked like a child.
I thought like a child.
Then, I grew from that child.

Into a man that stands
At any chance that is given
To make a difference,
Which is the purpose for my existence.

I was born to make a difference.
Born to have dominion.
Born to reign supreme
With the power that I was given.

And since Christ has risen
My sins have been forgiven.
No longer of this world,
I died to start living.

Walking in His kingdom
Is now my life's mission.
His kingdom is too great
For me not to witness.

If His kingdom's not first in your life
How can you live it?
You breath but you're dead in Christ
So what's the difference?

Trying to find your way in life
Through man's opinion,
When God's been the way and the light
Since the beginning.

Money's going to solve all your problems,
Are you kidding?
Think school is going to teach you
The meaning of kingdom living?

It's all about your character,
Righteousness in the spirit.
Love within your heart
Is all you need to live it.

Worries plague the world
But faith is there to cure it.
When you live a kingdom life
There is no need to fear it.

Stop with the excuses
And start moving forward.
If you can see it you can reach it
By simply walking toward.

Nothing is impossible
When you truly believe.
The ill became healed
And the blind can now see.

Storms have been calmed
And slaves were set free.
Seas have been parted
And blood was shed for me.

With all of that done
No creditor frightens me.
No boss stresses me.
No recession affects me.

I'm a child of the King
And the King's a good father.
Alone I made it far
But with him I'm going farther.

By walking in His kingdom
All of my troubles ceased.
He taught me to be humble
And gave my heart peace.

He showed me what mattered
And told me what didn't.
Like a child, I was lost.
But like the wise, I listened.

I have given many years
To what was unimportant.
Leaving was my fear
Because I thought it was important.

He told me not to worry
About food or what I wear.
If I put my faith in Him
All things I will bear.

Like the soul of Job
I triumph in the trial.
I fear God not the world
Because the world is vile.

The world can take my flesh
But it can't destroy my soul.
I can fall but I can't fail
Because it's His hand I hold.

And if it's His hand I hold
Then He is in control.
Nothing can trespass
Unless He permits it so.

And if He permits it so,
I must be ready for the challenge.
The dark side won't consume me
Because I'll bring the force balance.

I was lost as a child
Because I didn't have sight.
But as a man, I'm made whole
To walk a kingdom life.

To talk kingdom life,
To think kingdom life.
Because all is vanity
Outside the kingdom life.

STEPS TO SUCCESS

After coming to the realization of my existence, I mapped out the rest of my life. I sat down and wrote a plan that would free me from the shackles of the world and place me on a path to greatness. That plan consisted of the things I wanted to do and the necessary steps required to achieve them. Along with that plan I wrote out a budget. I didn't have much money, but with the little I had, I had to spend it wisely. With the plan well thought out, the only thing left to do was to act.

The first step taken was prayer. I asked God to guide me every step of the way. I also asked Him for forgiveness for not acting on the vision years ago when I first received it. Secondly, I approached my wife, Nikki, with the vision. Lying in bed, I told her about my dreams and how incomplete life would be if I did not fulfill them. Without hesitation or even a single mention of a job, insurance, bills, kids, or money, she said, "Go for it!."

Surprised to see how supportive she was, I asked, "Are you sure?" "Yes baby," she responded, "If that's what you want to do then do it. What's the point in life if you can't live it?" "You have a point," I responded ecstatically. "But do you understand that I'll be jobless for a short time?" She looked me in the eye and said, "No you won't. Your job is to pursue your dream. You may not be on the clock but you will be working. Regardless of what you thought I was going to say, I believe in you Tony. And if this is going to make you happy, I'm all for it." She rolled over, back facing me, and said, "Good night baby. Love you."

My wife has once again proven to me that she is a woman of virtue. While most women would've told their man not to quit their day job, she told me not to quit living. And for that I love her. And I write...

Virtuous *Woman*

What is a virtuous woman?
Her, who submits to the throne.
Her, who take burdens of the world
And by faith make right of what's wrong.

No matter how long the day
She still takes care of home.
As a loving wife and nurturing mother,
She is the back bone.

And with a faith so strong,
She's never down long.
No matter the tribulation
She still holds on.

The character of this woman
Is beauty within itself.
No need for finer things,
Her heart is her true wealth.

Unselfish in all her ways,
She is there to serve the people.
No act of discrimination,
All life is treated equal.

Kindness and integrity
Makes her love deeper.
The glow on her face
Shows God is her keeper.

The words on her tongue
Are loud but so peaceful.
Her attitude's angelic;
Strong, not lethal.

The man may be the head
But this woman is the strength.
Virtue is a blessing.
This woman is heaven sent!

The third step that needed to be taken was turning in my two week notice of resignation. When I returned to work the next day I made it top priority. I clocked in and waited for break time before marching to my supervisor's office to deliver the breaking news. When break time arrived I felt a strange sense run through my body. I quickly started chanting to myself a poem I'd previously written entitled, I Am. And I chant...

/ Am

I am not just a man,
I am a strong man.
I am a wise man.
I am what I am.

Blessings lay upon me.
Favor is upon me.
Grace be upon me.
Child of God, I am.

Everything I am
I work hard to be.
I aspire to be
The best that I can be.

The leader within me
Pours out when I speak
And when I am silent
A leader you still see.

I walk with authority,
Head held high.
Humbled in my ways,
Goals set high.

Ambitious I am,
You can see it in my eyes.
I am here to serve a purpose
Before my demise.

And before my demise
I will change many lives
With the seeds that I plant
Deep down in the mind.

I may not change all
But one is all I need.
One man to change his life
And change starts with me.

This poem eased my nervousness and uplifted my spirit all at once. I walked into my supervisor's office with confidence that everything was going to be OK. I sat the notice of resignation on his desk and told him October 2, 2008, would be my last day. I told him I was going to better myself and do what I was called to do. His response was, "It's a shame we're losing such a good man but it's great to know you're leaving with good reasoning. I wish you the best of luck with everything!" I walked out of his office and began to feel like a new man. It was like the weight of the world had been lifted off my shoulders.

THE LAST SHALL BE FIRST

Two weeks passed, and there I was looking at the last day of what I like to call corporate slavery. I was excited but afraid at the same time. Fear began to overrule my faith. I started having thoughts of failure, which brought on more thoughts of struggle and hardship. Yet I overcame the fear by thinking of the greats before me. Every great man or woman has encountered difficulty to some extent. Whether it be poverty, slavery, negativity, abuse, racial brutality, or just being on the wrong end of the stick, greatness came about. Greatness cannot be achieved without showing greatness on the path to greatness. I honestly believe God will strip you of everything just to show you how great you truly are. And I write…

STRIPPED

Stripped

God will strip you of everything
Just to bring you closer.
You will be molded until your attention
Is focused on the Beholder.

Everything you ever valued
Will be of little worth.
You will crawl on your knees,
Hands buried in the earth.

Friends will not know you.
Money will disappear.
Family will outcast you.
You will breathe fear.

Life will be hell,
Soon to be blessed.
The moment you surrender,
More is made of less.

Deciding to step out on faith and do God's

will required me to be ready for any barrier, or any obstacle that could break my focus. Therefore, I avoided as much negativity as I could. I rarely mentioned me quitting my job to anyone because most people would not understand my reason for doing so. People have a tendency of shooting you down quicker than lifting you up. They take shots at what they fear because they fear what they do not understand. But I understood that the key to success was never losing focus.

Walking into my job for the very last time, I took into account that the man who created the company stepped out on faith, believed in his product, and built a billion dollar empire from the back of his truck. After he passed, his children and grandchildren received his life's legacy as an inheritance. What makes me any different? What's keeping me from becoming legendary? What's keeping my children from an inheritance? These are the questions that drive me to excel. It was clear to me that life was much more than living from check to check. I am worth more than a few hundred dollars here and there.

On my last day, I clocked in with my head up and I told as many people as possible, "If you have a dream, live it. No ifs, ands, or buts about it. Live it!" Many people found out I was leaving on the day that I was leaving. They all questioned, "Where are you going? Do you have another job? What about your family? Isn't your wife pregnant? How will you survive?" People, wealth is where your mind is and survival is where your heart is, and mine are both in their correct place. When you truly believe in something and go after it with full determination nothing can stop you from achieving the impossible.

Now, there was one particular co-worker that I absolutely had to say good bye to before departing. She has supported me since the publication of my first self-published book and I would have been wrong to leave without doing so. I told her this was my last day at the company and I was going to focus on my dreams and aspirations. I said to her, "At the age of 23 I have accomplished much more than the average person would accomplish in a lifetime. I'm married. I have a son. I have a daughter on the way. Before turning 21 I've self-published three poetry books and traveled to surrounding cities to perform my poetry. Now imagine how far I could go if I did that full time. If I devoted forty hours a week to my dreams in the same manner I devoted to this job, imagine how much I could get accomplished." In amazement, she responded, "I can hear the passion in your voice. I know you will succeed. I'm so proud of you Tony. If I was young again, I'd do things a lot differently myself." "It's not too late," I interrupted. "As long as you have breath in your lungs and strength in your soul you can do anything you put your mind to."

I went on to tell her about a poem I had written for a high school black history program I was invited to speak at earlier that year. The students were predominately black and most lived in a "forgotten" urban area. As I waited to speak, I observed the students rude behavior and I honestly did not expect to be shown any respect. But I approached the platform with confidence, and the tables turned as I began to recite my poem. They actually listened and gave me a standing ovation at the end of it. That moment alone showed me that I could touch anyone, anywhere, at any time just by believing in myself. I asked my co-worker if she would like to hear it and excitedly, she said, "I sure would!" And I spoke...

Unchained

I stand before you today
Representing those who never could.
I stand proudly for my roots
For here, my roots never stood.

They fought hard for their freedom
But for them freedom never came.
Lincoln may have freed the slaves,
But blacks were still chained.

Chained down to the lynches
And hangings of Jim Crow.
Shot up and burned alive
While dangling from the rope.

All the blood shed
So that the future had hope.
All the lives taken
Because racist couldn't cope.

I stand before you today
Because long ago I wasn't allowed
To stand before a crowd
And preach the truth out loud.

So high praise to the King
For sending a Dr. King
To share with the world a dream,
Bringing change by one mean.

And that mean was sacrifice.
That mean was a great price.
In order to gain freedom
That price was one's life.

Many lives laid down
So we could walk the way we walk,
Talk the way we talk.
It was worth the battles fought.

But is the dream lost?
That's the question at hand.
Because we're striving to be thugs
Instead of striving to be a man.

We'd rather sell drugs
Than work with our bare hands.
We'd rather claim the hood
Than go and purchase land.

The chains have been cut
But our minds are still slaves.
You can't live in a new day
Operating in old ways.

We must change the way we think.
We must change the way we live.
We must learn there's more to life
Than making a dollar bill.

The problem that we have
Is not increasing wealth
but living beyond means
Trying to imitate wealth.

How can we get ahead
If we keep ourselves behind?
We shouldn't keep up with the Jones'
When priorities are out of line.

Tracing back through time
Negroes were dirt poor
So of course being the descendants
We yearn for much more.

Money's the objective
Get it by any means.
We'd kill our own brothers
Over shoes and expensive jeans.

We'd pimp our own women
Just to get green.
We'd slave night and day
Not to save but buy bling.

This is what four hundred years
Of oppression does,
When the captive is set free
Many will hold a grudge.

Few will forgive,
Others will be in rage,
Some will act in violence,
Little will behave.

The ignorant will be blind,
The wise will see it all.
The weak will fall short,
The strong will stand tall.

Well, today is the day
That we all stand tall,
Unbound from the chains,
And rise to the call

From when freedom rang
In every state and every city.
We must walk with dignity
To regain validity.

We have come too far
To simply stand where we stand;
Where they use to call us boy
Now they see us as a man.

Where they use to hose us down
For marching on free land
But now a black man
Can campaign to lead the land.

My God how times have changed
But we must change with it.
The mentality that we have
We must completely get rid of it.

Stop tearing your brother down
And start lifting your brother up.
If a man climbs a ladder
Help boost that man up.

Don't curse him with your tongue,
Speak highly of that man.
Don't hate on what he's doing
Instead support that man.

If you see a man in trouble
Don't ignore, help him out.
Because to love and serve others
Is what life's about.

What better feeling in the world
Than to know you made a change.
Depend only on yourself
When it comes to making change.

Because to see change,
It first must start with you.
When you encounter a problem
The solution is up to you.

Don't stand by and wait
For another man to lead the way.
Conquer your fears and take action
So tomorrow's a better day.

If freedom fighters would've waited
We'd still be segregated.
To see a change in this nation,
Their lives they dedicated.

And here we are letting rappers
Destroy a generation.
We'd rather be "trappers"
Than get an education.

Then blame the white man
For the problems that we're facing.
It's far from discrimination.
We're our own extermination.

We are the ones
That hold ourselves back
But it's time to man up
And take our minds back.

Pick up a book and read
So that you can learn something.
Because a man who knows nothing
Can only do nothing.

But a man who holds knowledge
Also holds power.
The civil rights was a great movement
But right now is our hour.

When you find something to die for
You find reason to live.
So let's discover our purpose
So our lives will be fulfilled.

This is the dream
All slaves had once dreamed.
To truly be free
And live by all means.

So by all means
Let's live in the dream.
With righteousness inside
Let's live life as kings.

I stand before you today
Representing those who never could.
I stand proudly for my roots
For here my roots never stood.

They fought hard for their freedom
But for them freedom never came.
Lincoln may have freed the slaves
But today we break the chains.

Smiling from ear to ear, she cheered and
applauded, saying, "Tony, that was soooo good! It's amazing
how you can remember all of that. And the message itself was
so true. I bet those kids looked at you like you were Dr. King.
You're doing the right thing by leaving this company to pursue
your dream. Many lives will be changed and many people
will be touched just by hearing your words. I wish you all the
best. You keep putting out poems like that and you won't have
to worry about working for anyone ever again." Her words
warmed my heart and gave me hope for tomorrow.

Many people believe life is all about getting a high paying
job that's going to create security for them throughout life.
I believe life is about using what you know and enjoy to the
best of your ability. I also believe in making wealth chase
me instead of me chasing wealth. If I do what I was born to
do than how could I not succeed? How could I not achieve
greatness?

Throughout my years of working for this prestigious
company, I learned that with good character, ambition,
determination, dignity, and integrity, one could move up to
higher status. Applying those same traits to personal life, one
could experience greatness. We simply have to set ourselves
free from the fears of the world and take a chance at life. We
must dare to dream. And I write...

SET FREE

Set Free

Yesterday we broke the chains.
Today we move ahead.
The future is awaiting.
We willingly have to tread.

We are free to feel alive.
Hope lies within the mind.
Don't succumb to your fears.
Climb over every time.

Life is what you make it.
Challenge yourself to dream.
Set no limitations.
Just reach and achieve.

Any man who can believe
Can accomplish anything.
Put faith into your work
And make real the unseen.

Unearth your potential.
Be all that you can be.
Give your life direction,
Rather living aimlessly.

Life is too important
Not to place a purpose on it.
Serve God, serve others,
That's the main purpose of it.

But in serving others
You should serve them with your gift.
A nine to five is good
But God made you more equipped.

Don't settle at a job
That ceases your true meaning.
Live life to the max
In the steps of succeeding.

Open up your mind
To the power that is vested.
Unclog your pool of dreams
That doubt has congested.

Step out into faith
And watch miracles unfold.
Persist and watch destitution
Turn into gold.

Poverty in a sense
Is a state of mind.
You can change your circumstance
When you first change your mind.

A man is what he thinks
And he does what he knows.
So whatever is on the brain
In reality is exposed.

If your thoughts are pessimistic
Progress will never show.
Shape your mind to think positive
And your character will grow.

One who remains stagnant
Will never see success.
But one who progress
Experience life at its best.

Why not take advantage
During your life's duration?
You can escape a world of ignorance
By gaining an education.

By finishing school
You can advance in what you do
But you don't have to finish school
To be the best at what you do.

Just confide within yourself
That you can be successful too.
If you chase your life's dream
Success will follow you.

Don't work for the money.
Make the money work for you.
When you do what you love to do
Money pours into you.

Stop stressing over bills
And start thinking of your future.
Grades you make in school
Don't necessarily make your future.

At any given time
Your life can transform
Where you start to see things
You wouldn't see in the norm.

Within a single moment
Your life is redirected.
Any flaw that you have
You can take and perfect it.

If ignorance is a plague,
Knowledge is the antidote.
If you can't attend a class
Read a book and take notes.

Many doors will open up
When you open your mind first.
New heights you must explore
If more is what you thirst.

Freedom is at hand
But yet two steps away:
Sacrifice and educate.
Be set free today!

I DREAMED A DREAM

The end of my work shift has arrived and

I am finally free to live life the way it is intended. Walking out
of the company doors I felt a breath of fresh air filling my soul
with happiness. I knew that tomorrow would be the first day
of a new life. The plan was written. The goal was set. And the
first few steps had been taken. The future awaited, and I was
ready to take on the world.

That night, I walked into my son's room as he slept in his
crib. I stood over him and placed my hand gently on his head,
and prayed. After talking with God, I spoke softly over my son.
"Malachi, you will grow to be great in whatever you may be
or do. The world is yours. Your life is in your hands, so make
it a great one. Anything you dream, just believe and achieve.
I support you and I love you. Good night." I walked out of his
room knowing that one day he would be able to look at the life

of his father and know that his father dared to be different by stepping out on faith and believing in a dream. He will draw inspiration from my life and begin to follow his own heart.

I thanked my wife, once again, for her love and support. And we slept, awaiting the promises of tomorrow.

That night I dreamed a dream. A dream that started in my childhood with my mother preparing me for an Easter speech. She made me learn it and recite it over and over till it became a part of me. She dressed me early Easter morning in a white suit and told me not to be nervous, that everything was going to be OK. The dream skipped forward, years into the future, and there I stood, prepared to speak at a university in front of millions of people. I opened my mouth and spoke...

STILL I DREAM

Still / Dream

Although I am free,
I still have a dream!
A dream that one day
We will walk like kings.

Not just Americans
But all human beings.
For this is the purpose
Of our very being.

To live our lives
To its maximum potential.
To die and be remembered
With honorary credentials.

A dream where ignorance
Is stripped from our mental.
And replaced with wise words
From the heart of the influential.

Today, I dreamed
Of dreams being achieved,
Fears being faced,
And success being decreed.

Champions arising,
And princes becoming kings.
A dream where all Man
Would fly on eagles' wings.

It has been foreseen
The potential we hold.
We have carried greatness
Since the threshold.

And since the threshold
We have struggled through a lot
But the struggle can't keep us
From seeing the mountaintop.

Today, I dream
We will conquer our fears.
A man is not a man
If he wallows in fear.

Life is not life
If it is smothered in fear.
How much more will you regret
By succumbing to your fear?

Fear of quitting your job
To make your own way.
Fear to do what you desire,
Why are you so afraid?

O, you of little faith
It is time to believe.
Set your heart on your goal
And you can succeed.

If it's happiness you want
Then utilize your mind.
If it's achievement you seek
Then sacrifice the time.

If it's fortune you're after,
Your mind's the gold mine.
If it's fame you desire
Then rise up and shine.

The freedom check's been cashed
So feel free to live.
Be the next example
Of a dream made real.

No matter the situation,
No matter the circumstance,
Greatness can come about
If only seen from a glance.

Every great man
Has to sacrifice something.
Success isn't free
So prepare to give something.

God gave His Son,
His Son gave His life.
To live out your dream
Will you lay down your life?

Will you break bad habits?
Will you cut people loose?
Will you live off of less?
Will you put faith to use?

What will you do
To see a purpose filled life?
It's time to stand up,
Give in, and sacrifice.

Stand up to your fear.
Give in to your dream.
Sacrifice any obstacle
Outweighing your dream.

Your dream is all you have
To unlock your true purpose.
Don't throw away the key.
Unlock your door to purpose.

Failure's not an option
If you can see success.
Focus not on the negative
But think for the best.

Give it your all
And when you're finished you can rest.
Have faith to step out
And God will guide you through the rest.

BEYOND THE DREAM

One month has passed and life is greater than ever. Change has taken place and the impossible has been made possible. Hope has been given to those in desperate need of it. Hearts have been filled with joy and happiness. Minds have been motivated to live life to its full potential. Eyes have witnessed a nations' history at its greatest. The people have voted. Change has come. The dream is fulfilled. And I write…

DREAM FULFILLED

Dream Fulfilled

From the dream of Dr. King
To the change Obama brings,
Vision is brought to life
Like books to movie screens.

Only, this isn't theatre.
This here, is the real thing.
Generations in the making.
Amazing Grace, we sing.

Here, we stand
To pay witness to the moment.
Today, history is made
As the Day of Atonement.

The impossible made possible.
The hopeless given hope.
A stepping stone for a culture.
"Yes We Can!" He spoke.

And yes we did with votes.
Votes we once couldn't make.
But my ancestors marched
In high hopes of today.

And on this very day,
The dream becomes real.
And by many measures,
The dream is fulfilled.

We've overcome police brutality.
We've integrated schools.
We've eaten in fine diners.
We've swam in public pools.

We've lodged in the finest
Hotels and motels.
We've been given fair trials
And not just thrown into jail.

We've become CEO's,
Lawyers, doctors, and politicians.
And to put a shining star
On Dr. King's bright vision,

Today, we witnessed
A dream made real.
President Barack Obama.
The dream is fulfilled.

On the fourth of November, 2008, we marched to the polls to make history happen. The world watched as America elected its first African-American President, Barack Obama. This not only set a milestone for blacks but for all minorities. The land of opportunity has finally lived up to its name. Watching America ascend to new heights is monumental within itself. One man dared to dream and bring change. Now, it is time for us to do the same. This nation is run by the people, so if the people do not change, neither will the nation. And I conclude…

DARE TO DREAM.

Going Beyond the Dream:
ADDITIONAL
POEMS.

Surrender

There is so much more required
Than what I'm presently giving.
I've gone through hell and high waters
But because of Love, I'm living.

So many trials and tribulations
That I've faced in my life.
So many things I did wrong
That I could've made right.

He said everything done in darkness
Will soon come to light.
I'm tired of living out of order.
It's time to make things right.

I dare not dream on
Still engulfed in sin.
A change is coming.
I can feel it burning within.

I lost focus long ago
But I'm back on track.
I have a seed on the way,
There's no time for lack.

It's time to suit up
And take my roll as a man.
The first step is to surrender
My life into Your hands.

God speak through me!

SURRENDER

PURSUIT

After observing my surroundings, I realize there are few people who know who and what they truly are and want in life. These people walk with confidence, talk with integrity, and live in ambition. They thrive off the success of their past and the faith they posses for their future. They never settle or become content. If they see opportunity for more they take it. It is not greed but advancement. As long as they have breath they walk with purpose.

In order to truly walk with purpose you must first walk in purpose. The walk begins by praying to the Creator, asking that your purpose be revealed; by putting your gift and talents to great use; by pulling out the potential within you; or by simply finding something to live and die for. What is it, by any means, you want to see happen in your life? One woman told me she only wanted to be happy. But what is it that has you unhappy? Could it be that you live day to day without any purpose or direction? When you walk aimlessly, you have nothing to look forward too.

Happiness has to be pursued. Once you have something placed before you that requires your touch, reach out and touch it. Do not sit there and stare as life drifts by. Reach for happiness. If you never attempt you will always fail. Failure is not of our nature. We were created to have dominion. Sure we may fall but it is not intended for us to stay down but rather get back up and learn from our mistake. Life without purpose is a true waste of existence. Seek purpose. Live to serve. Walk to lead. Hear to learn. Speak to inspire.

GRACE OF GOD

Grace of God

When I think of the grace of God
My soul feels the fire.
What other man do you know
Would die to take you higher?

What other man do you know
That can keep you from the fire?
Many men have come and died
But none rose like the Messiah.

Jesus came to save the souls
Of murderers, thieves, and liars.
Even Kanye West was blessed
Just to spit through the wire.

God doesn't discriminate.
He loves each and every one of us.
That's why when we do wrong
He makes it a point to punish us.

Like a parent to a child,
Do you see the connection?
He gives what we ask
But when we act He gives correction.

Disciplinary action
Just to shape us for perfection.
But fools hate correction,
That's why Jesus suffered rejection.

But how can you reject
A love that's there for you?
Through the good and the bad
He never abandons you.

When you're blessed with so much,
He still gives more to you.
When you're going through hell
And He pulls you through.

I don't know about you
But He has done a lot for me.
Things I can't explain or repay,
He only ask that I believe.

And obey His commands
That I may live eternally,
Peacefully, exceedingly,
And even more abundantly.

If that's all I have to do
To live life as a king
Then bring me my crown
Because I'm ready to be king.

I said it once before,
I am a king in my Father's eyes.
I don't have time to waste time
Drinking and getting high.

I don't have time to waste time
In the streets with gang riots.
There's too much purpose on my life
For me to deny it.

Too much potential on my life
To even think of denying it.
Satan talks a lot of game
So I just tell him be quiet.

I'm the head and not the tail.
He tempts but I prevail.
If you're not for me you're against me
So get on with all the hell.

Satan get behind me.
My God's an awesome God.
You can try me if you want
But my soul belongs to God.

So to God I give the glory.
To God I give the praise.
I'm walking in the kingdom
Because my debts have been paid.

I was able to rob the grave
By believing and getting saved.
So why complain about a job
When it's because of Him I'm getting paid?

All I did was kept the faith
That He would make a way.
But without work faith is dead.
So I worked hard to obey.

And when I started to obey
Life became okay.
If it wasn't for His grace
I wouldn't be here today.

Endure

I took my eyes off His kingdom
And my world fell apart.
The problems I had avoided
Came tugging at my heart.

Bill collectors calling,
I don't have the money for them.
My child wants to play
But stress stole my patience for him.

My lover won't love me
So I'm pointing to the curb.
Family keep calling,
They're all getting on my nerves.

The refrigerator's empty
And my tank is on E.
I can't make ends meet
Therefore I can't sleep.

My job is getting to me.
I hate it more by the week.
Suicide is on my mind
So I know my soul is weak.

But then I heard a voice saying
    It will get better.
    Don't give up in the struggle,
    Life changes like the weather.

But I've grown impatient.
I can't see pass the storm.
>Weeping may last for a night
>But joy comes in the morn.

>Everything you're going through
>In time it will pass.
Well how much longer Lord?
I don't think I can last.

>Speak life and not death
>There is power in the tongue.
>In the end you'll be awarded
>But the process just begun.

>Believe in my Son
>And let Him be your light.
>And you will not taste death
>But see eternal life.

I've strived to be righteous
But it's hard to stay focused.
>I never said it would be easy
>Just keep kingdom your main focus.

>Don't let your troubles break you.
>Instead let them make you.
>Endure through the night

And see where tomorrow takes you.

HIGHLIGHTS.

THE GALLANT MAN

What is it that makes me gallant in such troubled times? Faith!

The Gallant Man

...

We have been triumphant
Throughout the generations.
Marching tirelessly
Through hatreds infestation.

What was meant to stop us
Kept us pressing forward.
Many souls lost
But our pride was not lowered.

PROGRESSION

What is depression compared to oppression? What is
a temporary struggle compared to a lifetime of poverty?
Progression is demanded.

Progression

...

Tame the eye of lust
And control the spending hand.
Learn to live cheap
And preserve all you can.

...

Money should not determine
The character of our heart.
Poverty is a state of mind
And richness lies within the heart.

...

You were born to endure
The mishaps of time.
Molded to perfection,
Your potential is sublime.

P/\TH OF GRE/\TNESS

Greatness cannot be achieved without showing greatness on the path to greatness.

Path of Greatness

...

Dreams become real
When one stops procrastinating.
Don't hold yourself back
From something more fascinating.

...

You can be and do whatever
By believing you can make it.
Your dreams are your own,
Don't let anyone take it.

...

If success must be driven
How far will you go?
If the world runs on knowledge
How much do you know?

Stimulate your mind
And become your own boss.
The future's yours to gain
If you can pay the cost.

...

Why work for the man
When you can become the man?
Forty hours of your life
Is in another man's hand.

Forty hours of your life
You will never see again.
And your plan is to do this
Until your life ends?

...

How can life be fulfilled
When you don't fill the void?
You search for a meaning
But the answer you avoid.

You drive around in circles
Going where the money is
While passing your destination
Which is where your heart is.

PURPOSE

Everyday I pass people who view life from one perspective, conventional. As if they're still plugged into the matrix, they walk blindly through life, never living to their full potential... Finding and achieving purpose will fulfill your life in ways unimagined.

Purpose

...

Many people live life
Not knowing who they are.
They settle for what is given;
A false truth of who they are.

They may succeed in many things
And have ambition to go far.
But if they still lack happiness,
They're confused of who they are.

...

What gift do you possess
That could heighten someone else?
Purpose isn't about you
But enhancing someone else.

Advancing someone else
Is more awarding than any wealth.
Purpose is much bigger
Then succeeding for yourself.

...

If it's not in God's name
Then it is done in vain.
And if it's done in vain
It will go up in flames.

...

One's life is affected
By every action we choose
So make your purpose count
For all of those watching you.

...

We were not created
To be slaves to corporations.
The mission of our existence
Is to witness to salvation.

KINGDOM LIFE

As a child of God, it is my job to witness to the truth...

We are solely here to represent Him and enjoy the goodness of life...

By being hearers and doers of His word, we walk the kingdom life.

Kingdom Life

...

I was born to make a difference.
Born to have dominion.
Born to reign supreme
With the power that I was given.

...

If His kingdom's not first in your life
How can you live it?
You breathe but you're dead in Christ
So what's the difference?

...

It's all about your character,
Righteousness in the spirit.
Love within your heart
Is all you need to live it.

Worries plague the world
But faith is there to cure it.
When you live a kingdom life
There is no need to fear it.

...

I have given many years
To what was unimportant.
Leaving was my fear
Because I thought it was important.

He told me not to worry
About food or what I wear.
If I put my faith in Him
All things I will bear.

Like the soul of Job
I triumph in the trial.
I fear God not the world
Because the world is vile.

The world can take my flesh
But it can't destroy my soul.
I can fall but I can't fail
Because it's His hand I hold.

VIRTUOUS WOMAN

While most women would've told their man not to quit their day job, she told me not to quit living.

Virtuous Woman

What is a virtuous woman?
Her, who submits to the throne.
Her, who take burdens of the world
And by faith make right of what's wrong.

...

The character of this woman
Is beauty within itself.
No need for finer things,
Her heart is her true wealth.

...

Kindness and integrity
Makes her love deeper.
The glow on her face
Shows God is her keeper.

I AM

It was clear to me that life was much more than living from check to check. I am worth more than a few hundred dollars here and there.

I Am

Everything I am
I work hard to be.
I aspire to be
The best that I can be.

...

I walk with authority,
Head held high.
Humbled in my ways,
Goals set high.

Ambitious I am,
You can see it in my eyes.
I am here to serve a purpose
Before my demise.

STRIPPED

I honestly believe God will strip you of everything just to show you how great you truly are.

Stripped

...

Friends will not know you.
Money will disappear.
Family will outcast you.
You will breathe fear.

UNCHAINED

My culture has seen devastation in its worse form. We have
stared down the barrel of death and not even death could stop
us.

Unchained

...

Many lives laid down
So we could walk the way we walk,
Talk the way we talk.
It was worth the battles fought.

But is the dream lost?
That's the question at hand.
Because we're striving to be thugs
Instead of striving to be a man.

...

The chains have been cut
But our minds are still slaves.
You can't live in a new day
Operating in old ways.

We must change the way we think.
We must change the way we live.
We must learn there's more to life
Than making a dollar bill.

...

Tracing back through time
Negroes were dirt poor
So of course being the descendants
We yearn for much more.

...

We have come too far
To simply stand where we stand;
Where they use to call us boy
Now they see us as a man.

Where they use to hose us down
For marching on free land
But now a black man
Can campaign to lead the land.

My God how times have changed
But we must change with it.
The mentality that we have
We must completely get rid of it.

...

If you see a man in trouble
Don't ignore, help him out.
Because to love and serve others
Is what life's about.

...

Don't stand by and wait
For another man to lead the way.
Conquer your fears and take action
So tomorrow's a better day.

If freedom fighters would've waited
We'd still be segregated.
To see a change in this nation,
Their lives they dedicated.

And here we are letting rappers
Destroy a generation.
We'd rather be "trappers"
Than get an education.

Then blame the white man
For the problems that we're facing.
It's far from discrimination.
We're our own extermination.

We are the ones
That hold ourselves back
But it's time to man up
And take our minds back.

Pick up a book and read
So that you can learn something.
Because a man who knows nothing
Can only do nothing.

But a man who holds knowledge
Also holds power.
The civil rights was a great movement
But right now is our hour.

When you find something to die for
You find reason to live.
So let's discover our purpose
So our lives will be fulfilled.

SET FREE

… with good character, ambition, determination, dignity, and
integrity, one could move up to higher status…
We simply have to set ourselves free from the fears of the world
and take a chance at life.

Set Free

…

We are free to feel alive.
Hope lies within the mind.
Don't succumb to your fears.
Climb over every time.

Life is what you make it.
Challenge yourself to dream.
Set no limitations.
Just reach and achieve.

Any man who can believe
Can accomplish anything.
Put faith into your work
And make real the unseen.

...

Open up your mind
To the power that is vested.
Unclog your pool of dreams
That doubt has congested.

Step out into faith
And watch miracles unfold.
Persist and watch destitution
Turn into gold.

Poverty in a sense
Is a state of mind.
You can change your circumstance
When you first change your mind.

...

One who remains stagnant
Will never see success.
But one who progress
Experience life at its best.

...

Don't work for the money.
Make the money work for you.
When you do what you love to do
Money pours into you.

...

Many doors will open up
When you open your mind first.
New heights you must explore
If more is what you thirst.

STILL I DREAM

And while the world calls me crazy, I dare to dream.

Still I Dream

Although I am free,
I still have a dream!
A dream that one day
We will walk like kings.

...

A dream where ignorance
Is stripped from our mental.
And replaced with wise words
From the heart of the influential.

Today, I dreamed
Of dreams being achieved,
Fears being faced,
And success being decreed.

...

It has been foreseen
The potential we hold.
We have carried greatness
Since the threshold.

And since the threshold
We have struggled through a lot
But the struggle can't keep us
From seeing the mountaintop.

...

Life is not life
If it is smothered in fear.
How much more will you regret
By succumbing to your fear?

...

O, you of little faith
It is time to believe.
Set your heart on your goal
And you can succeed.

If it's happiness you want
Then utilize your mind.
If it's achievement you seek
Then sacrifice the time.

...

No matter the situation,
No matter the circumstance,
Greatness can come about
If only seen from a glance.

...

What will you do
To see a purpose filled life?
It's time to stand up,
Give in, and sacrifice.

Stand up to your fear.
Give in to your dream.
Sacrifice any obstacle
Outweighing your dream.

DREAM FULFILLED

Change has taken place and the impossible has been made possible. Hope has been given to those in desperate need of it... The land of opportunity has finally lived up to its name.

Dream Fulfilled

From the dream of Dr. King
To the change Obama brings,
Vision is brought to life
Like books to movie screens.

...

The impossible made possible.
The hopeless given hope.
A stepping stone for a culture.
"Yes We Can!" He spoke.

...

We've become CEO's,
Lawyers, doctors, and politicians.
And to put a shining star
On Dr. King's bright vision,

Today, we witnessed
A dream made real.
President Barack Obama.

THE *DREAM* IS FULFILLED.

For more coverage on
T.L. Black visit
PenmanPublishers.com

www.ingramcontent.com/pod-product-compliance
Lightning Source LLC
Chambersburg PA
CBHW071619040426
42452CB00009B/1400